KICKING THE
BUCKET LIST

DAYS	HRS	MIN	SEC
999	18	24	06

100 Downsizing & Organizing Things to Do Before You Die

by **Gail Rubin, CT**

The Bucket List Book Series

The Basic New Mexico Bucket List by Barbe Awalt (2015)

The Ultimate Hot Air Balloon Bucket List by Barbe Awalt (2015)

The Complete Cowboy Bucket List by Slim Randles (2015)

The Complete Space Buff's Bucket List by Loretta Hall (2016)

The Complete Santa Fe Bucket List by Pat Hodapp (2016)

The Complete Green Chile Cheeseburger Lovers' Bucket List by Barbe Awalt (2016)

The Ultimate Christmas Bucket List by Barbe Awalt (2016)

Kicking the Bucket List by Gail Rubin (2016)

Library of Congress Cataloging-in-Publication Data

Names: Rubin, Gail, author.
Title: Kicking the bucket list : 100 downsizing and organizing things
    to do before you die / by Gail Rubin, CT.
Description: Los Ranchos, NM : Rio Grande Books, [2016] | Includes
    bibliographical references and index.
Identifiers: LCCN 2016027922 | ISBN 9781943681150 (pbk. : alk.
    paper)
Subjects: LCSH: Storage in the home. | House cleaning. | Orderliness.
Classification: LCC TX309 .R83 2016 | DDC 648/.8--dc23
LC record available at https://lccn.loc.gov/2016027922

Front cover: Digital countdown clock. Courtesy of Wikimedia Creative Commons. Back cover: Courtesy of Gail Rubin.

CONTENTS

Buckets. Courtesy of Pixabay.

Foreword

"Because you are so busy, you do not notice you are dying," says the saintly Vietnamese Buddhist monk Thich Nhat Hanh.

We are bred to believe that staying busy and accumulating things will lead to a better life. As time goes by, we find ourselves surrounded by objects that no longer serve us or contribute to our enjoyment of life.

As for noticing death? We'd really rather not. Our fears start in childhood, as well-meaning parents seek to shield us from the inevitable by avoiding funerals. We work to create meaning from the lives we've been handed. We hate to hear that pesky inner voice whispering, "This too shall pass."

Downsizing and death may seem to be the ultimate killjoy. But, trust me, they aren't always deflating. We can get ready, live brilliantly and face the coming day with a renewed, collected, inspired spirit!

The keys to balancing all this are in your hands. Thanks to Gail Rubin's *Kicking the Bucket List: 100 Downsizing and Organizing Things to Do Before You Die*, staying busy while noticing that we are dying has a fresh, optimistic framework and a—what-do-you-know!—stunningly tangible pay-off.

Like martial artists in the "ready" position—strong, rooted, present to what is, and backed up by good memories of what came before—we can work these pages and accomplish a great deal with awareness. Reducing our excess goods, befriending death, and getting organized enough to proudly shake hands with it, improves our run-of-the-mill, day-to-day existence and helps us to better see life's magnificence.

In a workshop on bereavement, I was once asked to close my eyes and converse with Death. The Grim Reaper quickly appeared in long, dark robes, his bony hand grasping a scythe. "Why do you persist in wearing that ridiculous costume?" I asked. "Oh, you know," Death said in a surprisingly mopey tone. "I need people to take me seriously." What-ho! This opened my eyes. Death has a self-esteem issue!

This lovely, good-humored guidebook will help you take downsizing and death seriously, and lead you to give it a new costume. Follow Gail Rubin's clear-headed marching orders, culled from her extensive experience as a thanatologist and internationally-known death educator. You'll be able to get a handle on the stuff of your life, and release your attachment to burdensome objects.

Our families will be able to grieve more fully and grant us the send-off we most desire. They won't have to wonder what we would have wanted, where the car title is, or what our Facebook password might be.

There's still plenty to be busy with, and this "Kicking the Bucket List" is a beautiful start. Downsizing responsibly and planning for death is not just an exercise, it's a practice. If we do a little every day, week, month and year, we will deepen ourselves. We will see and feel more.

We can kick the proverbial bucket, and notice death in a new way. And the sunrises and sunsets will be a little brighter for this.

---AMY CUNNINGHAM

Amy Cunningham is a writer, lecturer, mom, wife, dog-owner, and New York state licensed funeral director. She maintains a funeral planning blog at FittingTributeFunerals.com.

Introduction

The term "kicking the bucket" is a euphemism for death with a rather grim origin. If a person wanted to end it all by hanging himself, he would rig up a noose around his neck, stand on an overturned bucket, then kick the bucket out from underneath to complete the act.

The term "bucket list" represents a compilation of things you want to do before you "kick the bucket." While I hope you don't plan to take that route toward death, there are great benefits to making a list of things to do before you die – especially when it comes to downsizing and organizing your life.

You don't have to be old or dying to downsize. When you've lived in the same place for a decade or three, stuff accumulates. We get attached to clothing, books, knickknacks, photographs, papers, all sorts of objects. Many of these things no longer serve us and become clutter.

It's a challenge to embrace simplicity. Few folks reach the level of hoarding, where your possessions crowd out the opportunity to live a fulfilling life or entertain guests in your home. That's living dangerously. Don't be like that.

While modern medical care has made great strides in extending lives, humans do still have a 100% mortality rate. Yet only 25 to 30 percent of adults do any end-of-life planning or preparation. That leaves 70 to 75 percent of the population unprepared and potentially devastated, not IF but WHEN there's a death in the family.

Are you telling your loved ones, "Don't have a funeral for me when I'm gone"? If they didn't love you, don't worry, they wouldn't go to the trouble. Assuming you do have some lovable qualities, do your family and friends a favor – decide how you want your carcass disposed of, make the arrangements yourself, sketch out some life celebration ideas, and tell those people what you've done.

The "Near Misses" list provides guidelines for the many follow-up activities that an estate executor has to tackle, whether the deceased person was organized or not. Other "Near Misses" that didn't make the Kicking The Bucket List follow, along with a listing of helpful websites. All of the websites listed at press time are viable. With the fluid nature of web pages on the internet, changes that lead to broken links may occur in the future.

The charity for this book is the National Hospice and Palliative Care Organization. Learn more about this outstanding organization on page 118.

A big thanks to Albuquerque author Steve Brewer, who has a wicked sense of humor. He suggested the title for this book. Many thanks to the individuals and organizations who helped make this such a stellar resource: the Intrepids Critique Group, for combing through the manuscript and suggesting edits; Stephen Hartnett with the American Academy of Estate Planning Attorneys, for reviewing the veracity of the Executor Checklist; funeral director Amy Cunningham, for her lovely foreword; and my husband David Bleicher, for being the Doyenne of Death's best buddy.

This book will help you become prepared for the day when you or a loved one will "kick the bucket." By tackling these downsizing, organizing, and preplanning items, you can reduce stress, minimize family conflict, save – or even make – money, and create a meaningful, memorable "good goodbye." Now, let's tackle this bucket list!

--- GAIL RUBIN
    Albuquerque, NM

100. Release Your Attachments

You can't take it with you. The Buddha observed that attachments are at the root of all suffering. Americans are really good at acquiring. We're not very good at letting go. We become anxious and stressed trying to hold on to people and products in a constantly changing world.

Attachment to stuff causes suffering. Our stuff represents our history, an accumulation that marks who we think we are. When we recognize change is constant, that all we really have is the present moment, we can learn to let go of our attachments to objects representing the past.

Letting go of those things that don't serve us, we can distance ourselves from the discontentment and dissatisfaction that stuff we don't love fosters.

Website http://www.aboutbuddhism.org/

The Buddha. Courtesy of Pixabay.

99. Liberate Yourself From Your Stuff

In 1990, I moved from Washington, D.C. to Albuquerque, New Mexico with only the possessions that fit into my Honda hatchback. I rented a furnished apartment and used those items for two years. It's amazing how little you need to live well.

We may move many times in our lives. With each move, we can reconsider which possessions to take. But when we stay in one place for decades, things accumulate.

As the phases of our lives progress, our needs and our clothing sizes change. Gifts from well-meaning friends may not resonate for you. Resolve to keep just those things you truly love, use, and can fit into.

Website: http://www.nextavenue.org/throwing-possessions-harder-think/

Moving Boxes. Courtesy of Pixabay.

98. Clear Your Clutter, Clear Your Mind

Clutter invites confusion. A cluttered space fosters turmoil and stress. An organized, welcoming home or office invites opportunities into your life.

It may sound "woo-woo," but many people swear by the magic of *fung shui*, the Chinese art/science of placement. Eliminating clutter is an important first step to allow good energy to flow through your surroundings.

Website: http://www.instituteoffengshui.com/house-and-home/clutterclearing.html

Oriental Doors. Courtesy of Pixabay.

97. Get Cats to Help Clear Your Clutter

When you adopt kittens, prepare to clear your clutter. Young cats are curious and amazingly agile. They will climb onto – and into – places you wouldn't believe. They will knock your knickknacks over. They will mess with the mail, magazines, and newspapers. The less stuff you have, the less kitty mayhem they can inflict.

Getting dogs can also prompt a pare-down of possessions. If the dog is big enough to wag its tail over the coffee table, at least keep that area clear.

Website: http://www.wayofcats.com/blog/cats-and-clutter-dont-go-together/31827

Cat. Courtesy of Gail Rubin.

96. Admit You're a Grown-Up

When you were a child, your parents probably admonished you to clean up your room. If your parents are still alive, the tables are turned.

Parents have accumulated decades of stuff, including things that their parents passed on to them. You – and your siblings, if you have them – will have to go through generations of photos, knickknacks, papers, and household goods after your parents die. Why not do this while they are alive?

Purging possessions, old documents and useless files before there's a death in the family will reduce confusion for the estate executor. If you dread the thought of going through your own files, imagine the increased burden of facing your parent's office files.

Website: https://unclutterer.com/2007/07/13/handling-inherited-clutter-part-1/

Knickknacks. Courtesy of Pixabay.

95. Give Yourself Time to Downsize

It takes decades to amass a significant amount of stuff. Don't expect to get rid of it all in one weekend. When my parents were downsizing from their home of 33 years to a three-bedroom condominium, it took months of work – including three yard sales and multiple donation trips to various charities.

If you're not in a hurry, six months is a good window of time. Tackling a small area for 30 minutes a day over six months adds up to 91 hours of downsizing. You can expend bigger chunks of time over a shorter period: one hour daily over three months yields the same time commitment – though perhaps more stress.

Website:: http://organizedhome.com/cut-clutter/declutter-101-where-do-I-start

Hourglasses. Courtesy of Pixabay.

94. Give Yourself a Deadline

While you want to give yourself enough time for the downsizing process, you also want to give yourself a deadline to get the majority of the work done. De-cluttering can be an endless task. Target a specific finish day, such as preparing for a holiday, birthday, anniversary, out-of-town guest visit or other special event. Deadlines provide a sense of both urgency and accomplishment.

Website: http://runningahousehold.com/?p=3339

Day planner calendar. Courtesy of Pixabay.

93. Evaluate Your Stuff

Take a critical look at your home or office. Do you love everything you see? Do you use everything you have? Are you overwhelmed with paper? Do you enjoy the way you are currently living? Do you cringe when you open certain closets, cabinets, drawers or rooms? Would you be comfortable having guests drop in unannounced?

Chances are, if you are reading this book, you have way more things than you love, use or need. The world will not end if you let go of objects cluttering your life. Start looking at your things and evaluating if they're worth keeping around.

Website: http://www.budgetdumpster.com/resources/how-to-declutter-your-home.php

Evaluate your stuff. Courtesy of Pixabay.

92. List What You Need or Don't Need

List-making can provide guidance as you decide what to keep and what to get rid of. Make a list of 100 treasured things you MUST keep. Make a list of 100 items you are tired of possessing. Your values become clarified as you list more items, helping to kick-start your downsizing adventure.

Website https://litemind.com/tackle-any-issue-with-a-list-of-100/

Young woman writing. Courtesy of Pixabay.

91. Focus on Joy

Consider the KonMari Method of clearing away clutter, created by Japanese professional cleaning consultant Marie Kondo, author of *The Life-Changing Magic of Tidying Up* and *Spark Joy*. She recommends focusing on how each item makes you feel. Does it bring you joy and make you happy? If not, why are you keeping it? Thank the item for its service and donate or sell it so someone else can treasure it. If it has no redeeming value whatsoever, recycle or trash it.

Website: http://tidyingup.com/

Smiley faces. Courtesy of Pixabay.

90. Take Downsizing Breaks

Sorting through your possessions and clearing excess objects is time-intensive and emotionally draining. If you're in the middle of a huge downsizing project, step away from the task at hand for a five minute break every hour. You can appreciate your progress when you come back refreshed.

Website: http://www.thewalledgardensstandrews.co.uk/blog/your-guide-to-decluttering-when-downsizing/

Tea Time. Courtesy of Pixabay.

89. Bring in a Friend

Friends can provide downsizing objectivity. Can't decide if your big shouldered jackets from the 1980s are worth holding on to? A friend can provide a fresh pair of eyes to help evaluate whether you really need to keep items of dubious value.

What if he or she advises you to donate things they secretly covet and offer to take items to the donation center for you? Just ask if there's anything they want and give it to them as a reward for their help. Then you won't be surprised to see your things at that friend's home on your next visit. Plus, when you take discards to make donations yourself, you feel lighter and get a sense of completion.

Website: http://www.wikihow.com/Declutter

Friends. Courtesy of Pixabay.

88. Keep a Clear Head

Clear the clutter in your mind to help reduce distractions during downsizing. Some tips: Write a list of tasks. Keep a journal. Avoid interruptions. Take a deep breath now and then.

Avoid downsizing under the influence of drugs or excess alcohol. This can negatively influence your judgment of an item's value. It can also trigger unhelpful emotional reactions. You might become clumsy and break objects, or even a part of yourself.

Website: https://www.realbuzz.com/articles/top-10-tips-to-clear-your-mind/

Too Much Alcohol. Courtesy of Pixabay.

87. Decide Your Approach

There are different ways to tackle downsizing. You can focus on specific objects, such as clothing, books, and papers, before addressing more sentimental items. You can focus on smaller territory, by addressing drawers, closets, shelves and cabinets. You could de-clutter one room at a time until the entire home is addressed.

To downsize in one huge effort, with assistance, you could choose the nuclear option – putting everything up for grabs in an estate sale. An estate sale expert will handle the pricing, advertising and management of the sale for a percentage of the proceeds. Set aside any items you truly want to hold on to before engaging the services of an estate sale expert.

Website: https://www.estatesales.net/companies/choosing.aspx

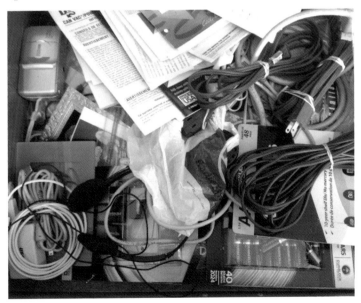

Stuffed Drawer. Courtesy of Gail Rubin.

86. Sort, Sort, Sort

One way to decide what to keep, what to donate, and what to discard is to set up boxes labeled for each action. Do NOT create a "maybe" box. Remember the OHIO rule – Only Handle It Once. At the end of each sorting session, process the contents as appropriate. This process can apply to just about everything: clothing, household goods, slides, photos, jewelry, letters, books, etc.

Website: https://www.caring.com/articles/downsizing-tips

Cardboard Box. Courtesy of Pixabay.

85. Stage Your Home

You don't have to actually sell your home to reap the benefits of staging your home for sale. Pretend you're going to sell your home and move. It helps you emotionally detach from your stuff. For a fee, a home stager will help you reduce your clutter, re-arrange the furniture, and spruce the place up. You may find you enjoy living in your "new" home so much, you don't need to move!

Website: http://www.hgtv.com/design/real-estate/sellers-
-the-benefits-of-staging-your-home

Lovely Living Room. Courtesy of Pixabay.

84. Appraise Art

There are many forms of art: paintings made with watercolors, oil, acrylic, and mixed media; prints made by lithograph, screen printing, and other techniques; photography; ceramics; and sculptures constructed of many different materials. You may have never heard of the artist, but their work might be selling for big bucks.

How can you tell if what you've collected, inherited or are preparing to sell is worth a fortune or a pittance? Turn to the experts at established, reputable appraisal organizations. Members adhere to a code of ethics, as well as the Uniform Standards of Professional Appraisal Practice. They charge an hourly rate, which can vary widely (i.e. $25 to more than $300/hour) depending on their experience and expertise.

Website: http://art-collecting.com/appraisals.htm

William-Adolphe Bouguereau (1825-1905) - The Wave (1896). Courtesy of Pixabay.

83. Appraise Jewelry

You may believe the jewelry you've inherited or plan to sell or insure is very expensive. But does the piece have real monetary value or only emotional attachment of no meaning to anyone else?

Until you have a qualified jeweler examine and appraise each piece, you won't know for sure. Make sure the appraiser is a professional qualified to appraise jewelry. They should be a graduate gemologist and affiliated with a national personal property appraisal organization.

Are the pearls natural or cultured? What's the setting made of? How does the clarity, color and cut affect the price of gemstones? Is the gold 24K? Valuations can affect estate taxes if the jewelry is worth many thousands of dollars. Have the jeweler report on the cash value at today's market rate. Then you'll have an idea of an equitable selling price, or a starting point to insure the jewelry.

Website: https://www.americangemsociety.org/find-an-appraiser

Jewelry Box. Courtesy of Pixabay.

82. Appraise Musical Instruments

Musical instruments can be quite valuable, yet many people sell them for pennies on the dollar, often unknowingly. Consider the person who bought an $8,000 player piano for $250 at a yard sale. Guitars, brass horns, violins, banjos (yes, even the much-mocked banjo), and other instruments may be worth a lot more than you'd think. Or, you may over-value a mass-produced instrument.

The only way to know the value of a musical instrument, either for legal purposes such as insurance, divorce settlements or probate, or to establish a valid sale price, is to hire an informed appraiser. They will charge a fee to provide a written appraisal.

Website: http://amis.org/resources/index.html

Violins. Courtesy of Pixabay.

81. Appraise Collectibles

Collectibles can have monetary value, or perhaps just sentimental value. For those who collect images and items depicting their favorite animals, such as owls, frogs, turtles, elephants, skulls, etc., chances are, the value is sentimental.

Modern day collectibles such as vinyl record albums, Hummel ceramics, baseball cards, Pocket Dragons, and other items may have monetary value, or maybe not. With antique collections, such as clocks, irons, toys, prints, furniture, advertisements, glass, pottery, etc., you can start getting into real money.

How can you tell for sure? Pretend you're on an episode of *Antiques Roadshow*. Take your treasures to an expert who can verify its authenticity and establish a value. But don't rely solely on an expert who wants to buy your items, as they may offer a lowball price.

Website: http://www.kiplinger.com/article/spending/T050-C000-S002-how-to-appraise-insure-and-sell-your-collectibles.html

Collectibles. Courtesy of Pixabay.

80. Appraise the House

Home appraisals provide an educated guess as to the actual value of your house. Banks and lenders need to know this figure to establish a collateral value for a mortgage loan. If you're selling the house, an appraisal provides a solid asking price. Appraisals also provide a starting point for obtaining a reverse mortgage, if you plan to stay in your house.

Appraisers will look at the conditions of a house's exterior structure, interior materials and quality, amenities and upgrades, and the front and back yards. They can also do sales comparisons, also known as comps, to get prices on similar homes in your neighborhood and recent market trends in the area.

Website: http://www.realtor.com/advice/buy/what-you-should-know-about-the-appraisal-process/

House. Courtesy of Pixabay.

79. Track Your Donations for Taxes

If you give items to qualified charities during your down-sizing spree, you may be able to take deductions against your income tax bill. The IRS permits deductions of the value of old clothes, furniture and equipment that are in "good condition or better." Making donations can be beneficial when tax time comes around. For example, if you are in the 25% tax bracket, a donation of goods valued at $1,000 may be worth $250 in tax deductions.

You'll need to get a receipt from the charity and list the items that you donate. Qualifying groups for tax deductible donations of goods include religious, medical, and educational organizations, community funds, and foundations.

Website: https://www.irs.gov/uac/Eight-Tips-for-Deducting-Charitable-Contributions

Calculator and Taxes. Courtesy of Pixabay.

78. Toss Your Own Stuff First

There's a story about Mahatma Gandhi, the nonviolent civil rights leader in India. He was a hero to a boy who ate too much sugar. The boy's mother brought him to see Gandhi after an arduous journey, hoping he could convince her son to stop eating sugar. Gandhi told her to bring the boy back in two weeks.

During that time, he himself stopped eating sugar. When the mother returned with her son two weeks later, only then could he tell the boy to stop eating sugar. Gandhi had to lead by example.

If you share your household space, your family or companions may not be as keen to downsize as you. If you start first, when the others see the beneficial changes in your surroundings, they may pick up the challenge soon thereafter. You can lead by example, just like Gandhi.

Website: http://www.soulcraft.co/essays/lead_by_example.html

Mahatma Gandhi. Courtesy of Pixabay.

77. Minimize the Multiples

If you belong to a warehouse club, you know how they bundle items together, or you're forced to buy one very large package. You really don't need to take up precious space with duplicates or giant-size items. If you regularly shop at warehouse stores and have the storage space, buying in bulk can be a smart move. If you're short on storage space, consider breaking up bulk purchases among your friends and share the savings.

Website: http://money.usnews.com/money/blogs/my-money/2014/03/18/15-items-always-worth-buying-in-bulk

Canned Food Multiples. Courtesy of Pixabay.

76. Cut Back on Christmas Décor

In the time B.C. (Before Cats), I had lots of Christmas decorations – dangly, sparkly objects hanging all over the house. Not any more, after one cat climbed on top of a cabinet and leapt up onto an indoor wreath that was hanging *over* a door, more than eight feet high! Those cute little crèche figurines make tempting playthings. Shiny glass ornaments are easily broken. Christmas stockings get pulled down.

Households with young children face similar challenges. You don't need a lot of stuff to have a festive holiday home. Unfortunately, so many pieces of Christmas décor have emotional strings attached, which makes them hard to release. Start downsizing by getting rid of anything that's broken or has negative emotional associations. Preferably prior to Thanksgiving, donate items you haven't used in a few years. Old lights can be recycled, too!

Website: http://www.simplyclearly.com/second-day-mini-malist-christmas-simple-christmas-decor/

Santa Candy Galore. Courtesy of Pixabay.

75. Reduce the Gift Wrap Reserves

Gift wrap, ribbons, tissue, bows and bags – how much do you really need? While you're donating Christmas decorations, donate most of your gift wrap supplies as well. They just take up valuable space the rest of the year. Experiment with more eco-friendly gift wrapping, such as fabric, baskets, tins and pretty boxes that may also be cluttering your home (see Regift Gifts).

Website: https://www.cityofmadison.com/streets/refuse/holidayWaste.cfm

Ribbons and Gift Wrap. Courtesy of Gail Rubin.

74. Regift Gifts

It's okay to pass along a new gift you may not be fond of, if it's perfect for someone else you know. Totally re-package the gift, to make sure you're not passing along someone else's gift tag to you or other incriminating evidence of regifting. To avoid embarrassing regift encounters, it's wise to pass those presents along to people in a different circle of family and friends.

Website: https://www.daveramsey.com/blog/10-rules-of-regifting

Gift or Regift? Courtesy of Pixabay.

73. Clear Out the Bathroom

Your bathroom has plenty of places to accumulate stuff: medicine chest, under-sink cabinet, over-toilet cabinet, and drawers. They may hide ratty towels, tiny bits of cleaning products, soap you hate, and over-the-counter medications way past their useful life.

Ladies, old make-up makes a prime downsizing target. Are you really going to wear that bright blue eye shadow again? Don't you know old mascara threatens your eyesight? Old foundation just makes you look like a pancake. Toss all makeup older than two years – it has expired.

Website: http://www.hgtv.com/design/decorating/clean-and-organize/decluttering-the-bathroom

Bathroom Cabinet. Courtesy of Pixabay.

72. Trim the Travel Toiletries

Do you really need all those hotel shampoos, soaps and hand lotions? Has the dentist given you multiple brand-new toothbrushes, dental floss, and small tubes of toothpaste? Have you picked up sewing kits, tiny emery boards, shoe shine pads and miniature packages of cotton balls and swabs? Put them to good use by donating these items to a homeless shelter or similar charity.

Website: https://unclutterer.com/2012/07/09/six-ways-to-repurpose-hotel-toiletries/

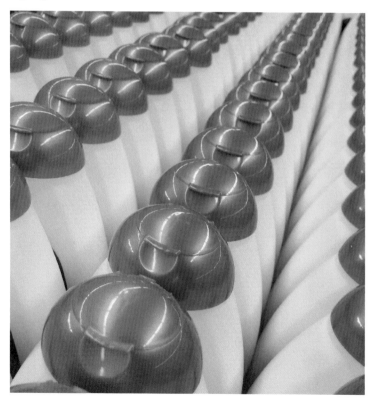

Travel Bottles. Courtesy of Pixabay.

71. Minimize Old Medications

It's tricky to dispose of expired prescription medications without polluting the environment. Flushing drugs down the toilet can cause groundwater problems downstream. Check with local government entities to learn your options for safe disposal. If there are no medicine take-back programs or DEA-authorized collectors in your area, follow these steps to safely dispose of most medicines in household trash:

1.   Mix medicines (do not crush tablets or capsules) with an unpalatable substance such as dirt, kitty litter, or used coffee grounds, so dumpster divers won't be tempted to put the meds in their mouths;

2.   Place the mixture in a container such as a sealed plastic bag;

3.   Throw the container in your household trash;

4.   Remove personal information on the prescription label of empty bottles or packaging; then dispose of or recycle the container.

Website: http://www.fda.gov/Drugs/ResourcesForYou/Consumers/BuyingUsingMedicineSafely/Ensuring-SafeUseofMedicine/SafeDisposalofMedicines/ucm186187.htm

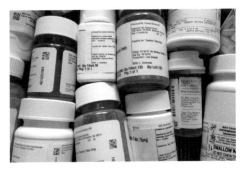

Prescription Bottles. Courtesy of Gail Rubin.

70. Cut Down on Kitchen Crap

Kitchen cabinets and drawers hide a multitude of clutter offenders: excess plastic containers and glass jars, a plethora of paper and plastic bags, gadgets and gewgaws. Almost everyone has a junk drawer, the repository of twist ties, rubber bands, toothpicks, straws, and mismatched plastic forks, knives and spoons. Really, when was the last time you needed any of those items? Reduce and recycle relentlessly.

Website: http://organizedhome.com/cut-clutter/save-time-cut-clutter-kitchen-declutter

Glass Jars. Courtesy of Gail Rubin.

69. Reduce the Rags

Honestly, how many pairs of old socks, holey underwear, and worn-out T-shirts do you really need for dusting? Do you even dust? Okay, maybe save a few pieces for cleaning your footwear. If you really dread throwing out these worn-out pieces of fabric, shred the cotton clothing for compost in your garden – but toss the polyester. Or investigate other creative uses for old clothing!

Website: http://www.ebay.com/gds/31-New-Uses-for-Old-Clothing-/10000000001471279/g.html

Rags. Courtesy of Pixabay.

68. Ban Business Cards

Nothing says clutter like business cards all over your office. If you want to hold on to the information in paper form, go Old School and revive the Rolodex®. Tape paper cards onto paper Rolodex cards in some organized fashion. Or, get rid of paper cards altogether! You can still save the information with a digital card file organizer such as the CamCard app (available in free and low-cost versions). It can help you reduce card clutter, enhance contact information and manage it all on your smart phone.

Website: https://www.camcard.com/

Business Cards. Courtesy of Gail Rubin.

67. Hold a Clothing Swap

If you don't like to let perfectly good clothing go to perfect strangers, consider a clothing swap. Invite your friends to bring clothing they no longer want to keep, and make a party out of trading cast-offs. What doesn't work for one person may be perfect for another. With food and drink, either provided by the host or the attendees, you've got yourself quite a festive event.

Any unclaimed items can be donated to charity. Just remember, the goal is to release your overabundance of clothing – not bring more home.

Website: http://www.womansday.com/life/work-money/tips/a1568/10-tips-for-hosting-a-successful-clothing-swap-107192/

Clothes on line. Courtesy of Pixabay.

66. Consider Consignment Shops

If your clothing or furniture is high-end and new or vintage/antique, consignment shops are one way to get cash for your goods. You keep ownership of your goods until they sell. If they don't sell, you take your stuff back. The shop gets a percentage of the sales proceeds. It's a relatively easy way to sell.

Or bring clean, good-condition clothing and accessories, new or vintage, to buy/sell/trade shops like Buffalo Exchange or Crossroads Trading Company. You may not get as much cash as you'd like, but you'll get more value in trade for store credit. They also offer sell by mail services.

Website: http://manvsdebt.com/second-hand-sales/

Mannequins. Courtesy of Pixabay.

65. Hold a Yard Sale

These are also known as garage sales, tag sales, and rummage sales. Pulling together these sales is a significant amount of work. You organize your goods, set them up for display, price the items, set up signs around the neighborhood, advertize in the local paper, start with change on hand, act as cashier, and keep the money secure.

People will paw through your stuff and offer much less than you've priced. It's an emotionally and physically draining experience to make a few hundred bucks. You might minimize your stress by having a friend or adult child run the sale while you go to the movies.

Do yourself a favor and donate the items that don't sell. Do NOT take them back into the house.

Website: http://www.yardsalequeen.com/yardsale.htm

Hats. Courtesy of Pixabay.

64. Sell at a Flea Market

Instead of holding a yard sale, pack up all the stuff you want to sell and take it to a local flea market. You pay a small fee for a space at either an indoor or outdoor location where sellers regularly gather. Take your own display tables and chairs to sit upon, and don't forget to bring cash for change! You skip having to advertise, but still have to round up your merchandise, haul it to the flea market, and haggle with buyers. Be prepared to play *Let's Make a Deal* with flea market shoppers. Plan to donate any merchandise that doesn't sell – do NOT take leftovers back home.

Website: http://www.fleamarketatmenge.com/flea-market/how-to-sell-at-a-flea-market/

Flea Market. Courtesy of Pixabay.

63. Sell Your Stuff Online

Selling your stuff online takes a commitment of time, attention and computer skills. In addition to eBay, the 800-pound gorilla of online sales, other popular online selling sites include Amazon, Craigslist, Etsy, and Bonanza. Selling items on Craigslist is free, while these other sites charge various fees.

eBay is eager to help you sell your items. With more than one million buyers, the company touts itself as the world's largest online marketplace. They make it sound so simple: "List it. Ship it. Get paid." It is a bit more complicated than that – you have to decide what to sell, take quality pictures of the item(s), price them well, package and ship the items to your buyers. Payments are made through a PayPal account, and the fees to eBay vary depending on how much you sell and the type of rate plan you choose.

Website: http://pages.ebay.com/sellerinformation/learn-to-sell-online/

Sell Online. Courtesy of Pixabay.

62. Give Your Stuff Away Online

Make it easy on yourself by giving away your items through Freecycle. The Freecycle Network® is made up of more than five thousand groups with more than nine million members around the world. It's a grassroots and entirely nonprofit movement of people who are giving – and getting – stuff for free in their own towns.

Freecycle focuses on reusing and keeping goods out of landfills. Each local group is moderated by local volunteers and membership is free. To sign up, find your community in the search box at Freecycle.org.

Website: www.FreeCycle.org

FreeCycle website screen grab. Courtesy of FreeCycle.org.

61. Make Charitable Donations

Charitable organizations will pick up or accept a majority of gently used household goods, although many won't accept old televisions, mattresses, computers, and some furniture. They especially appreciate automobile donations. To avoid shipping costs, donate to local charities. Keep track of what you donate. The organization will give you receipts that serve as proof for tax deductions. Popular charities that may pick up donations from your home include Goodwill, the Salvation Army, ARC, Vietnam Veterans, Big Brothers Big Sisters, and others.

Website: http://donationtown.org/

Salvation Army Disaster Service Truck in Iowa. Courtesy of Wikimedia Creative Commons.

60. Help Habitat for Humanity

If you have unused building materials, Habitat for Humanity will take them. They use materials to construct decent, safe affordable housing. Or, they may raise money by selling your donations in their thrift stores. Habitat for Humanity offers a great outlet to donate tools, cabinets, doors, light fixtures, furniture, and other items. They can recycle sinks, toilets, tubs, serviceable water heaters and furnaces, and other items taken out during a home renovation.

Website: http://www.habitat.org/

Habitat for Humanity Build, Las Cruces, New Mexico. Courtesy of Habitat for Humanity New Mexico.

59. Donate Discards for Pets

Dog or cat lovers, consider donating household goods, automobiles, and unused pet toys, treats and care items to your local Animal Humane Society, other animal welfare groups or your municipal animal shelter. Some shelter organizations, but not all, will take old towels and sheets for animal bedding.

Website: http://www.animalcharityevaluators.org/recommendations/list-organizations/

Sleeping Dog. Courtesy of Pixabay.

58. Love Your Local Libraries

Are you really going to read all those books? Many public libraries will gladly take your excess books, as well as DVDs, CDs, VHS tapes and records (check their value first), to sell at a fundraiser or possibly put into circulation. Depending on the library, your donation may be tax-deductible.

You might divide your books up and give religious books to church or synagogue libraries, large print books or popular titles to the libraries in retirement/assisted living communities, books for kids to elementary schools, or scholarly titles to special collections at universities. Make sure to check there's nothing stuck inside the pages that you'd want to keep – like money!

Website: http://www.ala.org/tools/libfactsheets/alalibrary-factsheet12

Library book shelves. Courtesy of Wikimedia Creative Commons.

57. Think of Theater Groups

Local theater groups can use vintage clothing for costumes. Set designers need furniture and art. Household items make great props for sets. If you are a fan of theater productions, reach out to your favorite thespians and offer your goods. You might also check with your local high school's drama department. Chances are, they'll be happy to take them.

Website: http://www.props.eric-hart.com/resources/the-100-best-sites-for-the-prop-maker/

Theater Production. Courtesy of Pixabay.

56. Curb Your Stuff

Put your items out on the street with a "FREE" sign! They may disappear within hours. Some people actually cruise streets looking for these opportunities. However, if it doesn't disappear within a day, don't let it languish out on the sidewalk. You wouldn't want to be cited for littering.

Website: http://plungedindebt.com/curb-watching-and-ways-to-get-free-stuff/

Free Sign. Courtesy of Pixabay.

55. Give Eyeglasses a New Life

You probably have more than one old pair of prescription eyeglasses you never wear anymore tucked away in a drawer. Give those glasses a new life with Lions Club International's program, Lions Recycle for Sight.

They collect old eyeglasses throughout the year, sort them by prescription strength, then clean and repackage them. They are given to people in need in developing countries. Clean out your drawer and help people see better! Your eye doctor or optician may know where the nearest collection boxes are located.

Website: http://www.lionsclubs.org/EN/how-we-serve/health/sight/eyeglass-recycling.php

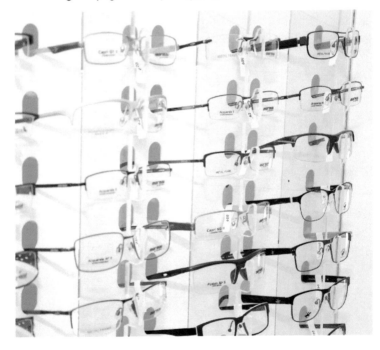

Eyeglasses. Courtesy of Pixabay.

54. If It's Broke, Don't Fix It

When something breaks, you don't have to fix it. Those items may be telling you it's time to let them go. Our elders who lived through The Great Depression would fix things because they didn't have money to buy new, and they didn't have much stuff to clutter their lives. If clutter is an issue for you, when clothing, appliances, china, knickknacks and other items break, just get rid of them. Really, it's okay.

If you are a crafty type of person and would get great joy out of re-purposing broken items, have fun turning broken household items into unexpected art.

Website: http://www.diyncrafts.com/6081/repurpose/100-ways-repurpose-reuse-broken-household-items

Broken down vehicles. Courtesy of Wikimedia Creative Commons.

53. Recycle Relentlessly

With all of this discussion of getting rid of paper, plastic, glass, and metal, please remember to be kind to the environment during your downsizing. Recycle everything that your local municipality will accept. If you have curbside pick-up of recyclables, it's even easier than having to haul materials to a collection center.

Some odd things can be recycled: small appliances and electronics, pots and pans, plastic toys, and books. Take advantage of computer/big electronic recycling events. And remember, you can get paid for recycling aluminum cans, if you take them to a collection center that buys aluminum.

Website: http://www.wm.com/thinkgreen/what-can-i-recycle.jsp

Think Green. Courtesy of Waste Management.

52. Handle Hazardous Household Waste Properly

Most municipalities require special treatment of hazardous waste disposal, including paints, solvents, pesticides, chemicals, and automobile fluids. Check with your local public works department for guidance. Some hardware stores collect and recycle batteries and CFL bulbs, also considered hazardous waste.

A professional painter provided this tip for neutralizing leftover paints: mix these hazardous liquids with kitty litter - it turns paint into a solid waste. Once the material has hardened overnight, it should be okay for disposal in your ordinary trash.

Website: http://www.wikihow.com/Dispose-of-Hazardous-Waste

Paint Cans. Courtesy of Pixabay.

51. Stop Junk Mail

Have no interest in the junk mail you get? Put it into the recycling bin or trash as soon as it arrives. To reduce the amount of junk mail you get, contact the Direct Marketing Association's (DMA) Mail Preference Service and ask that your name be removed from mailing lists. The fee for this service is $1.00. There's a web form you can use to register online. Because some mailings are prepared far in advance, allow 30-90 days for your registration to become fully effective.

Not online? Send the following information, with your $1.00 check payable to DMA, to Mail Preference Service, PO Box 282, Carmel, NY, 10512: First name, middle name, last name; Address (including apartment number, if appropriate); City, State, Zip code; E-mail address (if you have one).

Website: https://www.dmachoice.org

No Junk Mail. Courtesy of Pixabay.

50. Stop Subscriptions

Getting mailed magazines and newsletters you don't read? Stop the slaughter of defenseless trees by stopping those subscriptions. Most magazines offer cancellation options by phone, mail or Internet.

Look at the publication's masthead, the page where the editors, contributors and advertising contacts are listed. Cancellation information is usually listed there. Have your billing information or account number from the mailing label handy before calling customer service. You might even be able to recoup some of your subscription fees.

Website: http://www.ehow.com/how_2334870_cancel-magazine-subscription.html

Magazines. Courtesy of Pixabay.

49. Empty Your Storage Units

Did you rent a storage unit to "temporarily" store some must-keep items that didn't have a place in your home? Depending on the provider, self storage units can range from $50 a month for a 5'x5' space to $300 or more for a 10'x30' space. Multiply that by 12 months and you're spending $600 to $3,600 a year on stuff you are not using. Take a hard look at what's in those storage units. Are those items even worth that rent? Clear out the storage unit, close the account and save yourself some money.

Website: http://www.slate.com/articles/arts/culture-box/2005/07/selfstorage_nation.html

Storage Unit Doors. Courtesy of Pixabay.

48. Clear the Out-of-the-Way Areas

Apartment dwellers generally don't have to worry about stuff collecting in the basement, the garage, the attic, a storage shed or a junk room, because they don't have those spaces to fill. Some apartment buildings have a communal storage space in the basement for sporting goods and lawn chairs.

Homeowners naturally fill these out-of-the-way spaces over time with junk, just as river sediment gets deposited when water flows downstream. Pull everything out, thoroughly clean the space, and be ruthless about cutting back on what stays. If it hasn't been used in a year, or you don't know what it's for, let it go. Organize and label the stuff to be kept – and use it.

Website: http://www.zillow.com/blog/basement-attic-garage-storage-178348/

Attic Storage. Courtesy of Pixabay.

47. Tackle Your Technology

Within our lifetimes, music media has gone from vinyl, to tapes, to CDs, to digital files – and in 2016, for some, back to vinyl records. Our home movies have gone from 8mm film, to VHS tapes, to DVDs to digital video, and some film-makers now love the retro look of 8mm. How do you decide what to keep and in what form?

If you don't have the technology to play the media, but you still want the sounds and the images, it's time to digitize. Digital music takes up no space at all, and it can be accessed through many different platforms. Businesses can transfer your music and films/videos to media files for a reasonable cost. You might even find a film-maker who wants to buy your old family films!

Website: http://www.kiplinger.com/article/real-estate/T057-C000-S002-how-to-digitize-your-photos-movies-and-music.html

Records and VHS Tapes. Courtesy of Pixabay.

46. Prune Back the Photographs

Getting rid of old photos, as well as new digital photos, is one of the hardest things to do – they have such emotional resonance in our lives. Consider these ideas to make the process easier. If you don't recognize the people in the pictures and relatives can't identify them either, toss them. If they are less-than-artistic images of landscapes, toss them. If they're out-of-focus, seriously damaged, duplicates, or feature people who bring up bad memories, toss them.

Going through old photos with an elderly relative can provide a helpful trip down memory lane, for both you and that older person. Take notes on stories you learn and mark significant photos. You'll still have plenty of images you'll want to keep – which brings us to our next Bucket List item.

Website: http://practicalarchivist.com/please-delete-digital-photos/

Sorting Photographs. Courtesy of Pixabay.

45. Digitize What You Can

Digital technology enables you to save music, videos and photos without taking up physical space. You can scan images and make virtual photo albums that can be easily shared with family members by email, online or on a thumb drive. All your CDs can be transferred to computer files – still accessible for listening, but not taking up space on your shelves. Family films or videos can also be transferred to digital formats – perhaps the next YouTube sensation is hiding in a closet!

You might consider using the website LifePosts, an online repository for your digital memories. They offer easy-to-use storytelling tools that enable you to create beautiful memorials, wedding anniversary albums, and digital keepsakes for all of life's important milestones. And you can collaborate on stories, share them selectively, and preserve those stories in perpetuity online.

Website: https://www.lifeposts.com/

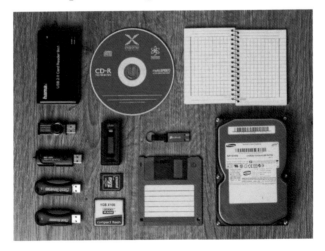

Digital Media Options. Courtesy of Pixabay.

44. Forgo Some Furniture

Did you combine households with your sweetie and put all the furniture from two homes into one place? Maybe you inherited a castoff sofa and chairs from a downsizing relative? Is that old lounger looking really abused? There is such a thing as too much furniture. Give away or sell some pieces and open up your space.

Website: http://www.getridofthings.com/household/get-rid-of-old-furniture/

Furniture. Courtesy of Pixabay.

43. Talk About Your Stuff

If you feel very strongly about wanting to keep a specific item, there must be a story about it. Talk to your loved ones about these things. Tell the stories these objects hold. Why is this an important article? If an object doesn't have a story, it's just another piece of rubbish to donate, recycle or trash. Talking about your treasured items can help you process your life experiences, make meaning, and share memories.

Website: http://learning.blogs.nytimes.com/2014/09/30/what-objects-tell-the-story-of-your-life/

Objects Have Stories. Courtesy of Pixabay.

42. Label Objects

There are lots of reasons to label the objects you choose to keep. Labels can indicate who gets what when the estate is being distributed. However, this approach is not legally binding. To do so, make a written list of items, to whom each item would go, and sign and date the list. Then, reference this list in your will and/or trust documents.

Labels can explain why something is significant – its age, what it cost when purchased, whether the artist is famous, etc. Label the people in scrapbooks – you think you'll remember names, but in truth, you won't remember many of them 30 years down the road.

Website: http://www.nytimes.com/2010/09/05/magazine/05FOB-Consumed-t.html

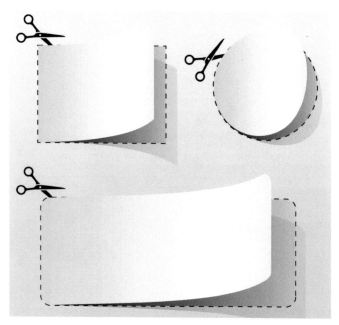

Labels. Courtesy of Flickr.

41. Don't Keep Relatives' Stuff

Objects get passed along from parents to children, from sibling to sibling, from grandparents, aunts and uncles to grandkids and cousins. Unless these items are really wanted, don't feel like you have to hang onto them.

To avoid generating hard feelings, be discreet. Don't let the giver know that you've passed those objects on to another deserving person or put them in the recycling or trash bin. If you're asked about an object, just say you've put it in a safe place and change the subject.

Website: https://www.caring.com/blogs/caring-currents/how-to-clean-out-parents-house-and-get-rid-of-junk

Clutter in Shed. Courtesy of Pixabay.

40. Give Family Heirlooms Now

If you plan to give heirlooms and family treasures to specific family members, give those gifts to them today, while you can see the look of pleasure (or pain) on their faces. If these heirs insist they don't want those items, you can change your gifting plans. Perhaps local historical societies and deserving nonprofit organizations can benefit from these heirlooms.

Website: https://unclutterer.com/2007/07/02/family-heirlooms-give-them-away-at-milestone-celebrations/

Berend van Iddekinge (1717-1801) with his Wife Johanna Maria Sichterman (1726-1756) and their Son Jan Albert (b 1744), Philip van Dijk, 1744-1748. Courtesy of Pixabay.

39. Get Organized for End-of-Life Issues

If you've actually been doing these Bucket List items, you've cleared out your excess goods. Now it's time to focus on end-of-life organizing. Fear of death is why more than 70% of adults don't make these arrangements. They think, "If I do these things, death will happen sooner" or "I'm not ready to do this yet. I've got time."

News Flash – Humans have a 100% mortality rate, and we never know when that last day will come. It's going to happen whether you plan or not. Tackle the rest of these Bucket List items so your loved ones won't have to scramble to gather vital information and make expensive decisions under duress of grief.

Website: http://agoodgoodbye.com/news-and-notes/resolving-to-get-end-of-life-organized/

Organize Your Information. Courtesy of Pixabay.

38. Sit Down With a Certified Financial Planner

Before making any major moves, evaluate your financial situation with a Certified Financial Planner (CFP). These individuals meet rigorous professional standards and have the education, experience and ethics to help you make the most of your finances from here to eternity. If you have champagne taste and a beer budget, he or she can help you find the balance between your desired lifestyle and how you'll pay for it.

Website: http://www.letsmakeaplan.org/choose-a-cfp-professional/find-a-cfp-professional

Piggy Bank. Courtesy of Pixabay.

37. Consider a Reverse Mortgage

People aged 62 and older who live in their homes as a primary residence and have equity in their homes can take out a reverse mortgage. Instead of you paying the mortgage company, the mortgage company pays you, using the equity in your home as collateral. The amount you can get depends on your age, the appraised value of your home, the current interest rates, and how you take the payment.

While it's a loan, you don't have to pay it back as long as you live in your home. However, payback is expected after the homeowner(s) die(s). Heirs who expect to receive money from the sale of the folks' home may receive very little. In some cases, reverse mortgage money can be used to provide a benefit to heirs through life insurance. Reverse mortgages can be expensive and complex, so do your homework before taking the plunge.

Website:http://portal.hud.gov/hudportal/HUD?src=/program_offices/housing/sfh/hecm/rmtopten

House. Courtesy of Pixabay.

36. Don't Wait Until It's Too Late to Move

Moving takes a lot of energy, and even the smoothest transitions can be very draining and stressful. If you are considering relocating into an independent or assisted living facility, do it while you are still mentally and physically able to look at these places and ask pertinent questions. Can a pet live with you and do they limit the size or type of animal? Is there a large "buy-in" investment to get in? What happens if you outlive your money?

Look for a living arrangement that offers on-site health care options, such as a rehabilitation or an intensive care wing. You won't have to go somewhere else to recover if you have an accident or fall in your retirement home/apartment. You can do rehabilitation exercises and therapies where you live.

Website: http://www.aplaceformom.com/blog/2013-3-11-signs-its-time-for-assisted-living/

Man With Suitcase. Courtesy of Pixabay.

35. Look at Escalating Care Options

Another consideration for those looking at moving to a retirement community: find a place that offers greater levels of service as needs increase. Independent living may evolve to assisted living, to nursing care, or to "memory care" if someone develops Alzheimer's disease. When a retirement community offers these services, you can avoid a wrenching move at a most vulnerable time.

Website: http://newoldage.blogs.nytimes. com/2008/10/20/10-things-to-know-about-assisted-living/

Assistance. Courtesy of Pixabay.

34. Make Auto Arrangements

What if disabilities end your ability to drive? What will happen to your automobile after you die? You can make a tax-deductible donation of the vehicle to benefit a nonprofit organization, such as your local public radio or TV station, or any qualifying charity of your choice. They take the automobile away and give your estate a generous tax break.

If your car is leased, the estate may be responsible for paying fees related to breaking the lease. The company may make a claim against the estate for outstanding funds. Consult an attorney about your rights.

You could give vehicles to family members through your will. Your executor can sell the car and put the proceeds into the estate. Your guidance while you are still alive can go a long way to help your survivors know what to do.

Website: https://www.irs.gov/pub/irs-tege/pub4303.pdf

Classic Ford. Courtesy of Pixabay.

33. Write Your Family History

Family histories often are passed down orally from generation to generation. At some point, the details become hazy. Names, dates, relationships and places are forgotten. Before too long, second cousins aren't sure how they're related exactly. So, it's valuable to write these stories for posterity.

It doesn't have to be elaborate – recording the branches of the family tree is a good way to start. Adding the livelihoods and locations for these relatives, their spouses and their children can create a simple family history picture. Or, dictate the information you know in an audio or video format. Curious family members may be inspired to investigate and document further.

Website: https://familysearch.org/wiki/en/Create_a_Family_History

Family History Books. Courtesy of Pixabay.

32. List Your Online Passwords

Having an online/digital life means you have to remember a lot of different passwords for different accounts. There are codes for your electronic devices, and passwords galore: for emails and social media, bank and credit card accounts, shopping websites, electronic health records, news websites, investment accounts, hotel and travel websites, on and on!

Some websites want you to change your password every three months. You probably have different user names on different accounts. How will you remember all of this information? Write it all down in a spreadsheet or word processing document you can update periodically, keep it in a safe place, and tell your executor about it. You can write updates on the printout.

Or, you can take a chance on the security of those online password protection sites that only require one master password. Just don't forget that master password, and remember to update log-in changes.

Website: http://www.wired.com/2016/01/you-need-a-password-manager/

Passwords. Courtesy of Pixabay.

31. Recycle Old Paper Files

Don't confuse your executor with non-essential papers in your personal or office files. Get rid of papers related to properties you no longer own and expired insurance policies. Minimize excess papers that have no current value.

Shred documents with sensitive information, such as Social Security numbers and medical records. Check this online article for guidelines about keeping vital records, legal papers, and tax returns.

Website: http://www.apartmenttherapy.com/drowning-in-paper-what-to-keep-what-to-toss-what-to-digitize-201044

Shredded Papers. Courtesy of Pixabay.

30. Make a Master File of Important Papers

You can help your loved ones by putting important papers together in one place and letting them know where it is. These papers could include will, trust and advance medical directive documents, birth and wedding certificates, veteran and Social Security papers, annuity and insurance policies, deeds, financial accounts and other assets, family and friends contact information, online passwords, etc.

Depending on the complexity of your financial life, this Master File could be a three-ring notebook binder, a dedicated fireproof box, with or without a lock (don't lose the key!), an accordion file folder, or a filing cabinet drawer. To help you pull all these important papers together, visit www.AGoodGoodbye.com and download the free planning form at the site's home page.

Website: http://agoodgoodbye.com/

Master File. Courtesy of Pixabay.

29. Write Your Advance Medical Directives

If everyone went directly from healthy to dead, we wouldn't need advance medical directives. Even if you don't want it, today's technology can keep you alive.

An advance medical directive spells out your medical wishes in writing, giving loved ones life and death guidance. It speaks for you when you can't speak for yourself – say, if you're in a coma or have Alzheimer's disease.

The Five Wishes form from AgingWithDignity.org is a plain-language, low-cost option that's legally recognized in 42 states, used in all 50, and available in 28 languages. You can dictate how you want to be treated at end-of-life – the setting, people present, and physical treatment you'd like. My favorite is to be massaged with warm oil – don't wait until you're dying to get a good massage!

Website: https://agingwithdignity.org/

The Five Wishes Form. Courtesy Aging with Dignity.

28. Name Your Durable Power of Attorney for Healthcare

Make someone with a strong backbone your Durable Power of Attorney (POA) for Healthcare Decisions, also known as a health care proxy. This person knows your medical care wishes and will carry them out when you can't speak for yourself. The advance medical directive document gives your spokesperson the authority to make decisions regarding your care, including the withholding or withdrawal of life-prolonging treatment. Most states require this document signing to be witnessed and notarized.

Take this document with you whenever you go to the hospital or on a trip. Online services like DocuBank.com can make your medical wishes available to medical facilities anywhere in an electronic format. This document should be reviewed and updated every three to five years. If your marital status changes, you wouldn't want an ex-spouse making these kinds of important decisions for you.

Website: https://www.americanbar.org/content/dam/aba/uncategorized/2011/2011_aging_hcdec_univhcpaform.auth-checkdam.pdf

Doctor. Courtesy of Pixabay.

27. Establish a Financial Power of Attorney

A financial power of attorney, also known as a Durable Power of Attorney (POA) for Finances, is naming a trusted person you name to carry out financial transactions on your behalf should you become incapacitated or demented. The financial POA and the medical POA can be the same person.

A financial POA may be given authority to do whatever monetary transactions you would do yourself if you could. This agent is required to act in your best interests, maintain accurate records, keep your property separate from his or hers, and avoid conflicts of interest. You can name a secondary agent, should your primary choice become unavailable. The financial POA's authority ends when you die – at that point, the court-appointed executor of your estate becomes the responsible agent for your financial affairs.

Website: https://www.caring.com/articles/how-to-set-up-power-of-attorney-for-finances

Money. Courtesy of Pixabay.

26. Identify an Executor

Before you name an executor for your estate, also known as a personal representative, consider the people you know who are organized, trustworthy and financially savvy. Being an estate executor is a big responsibility, one that may take years to fully complete. This is the person who, after your death, will be appointed by the court to handle all your affairs. He or she will pay all your outstanding bills, file your last tax return, and work with your attorney, accountant, investment advisor, insurance agent and others to settle your estate.

They need to keep organized records and detailed notes about all the time they spend on settling your estate. If the job seems too daunting to do for free just because you were good friends or close relatives, know that executors can charge the estate an hourly rate for their work on your behalf, or get a lump sum payment.

Website: https://unclutterer.com/2014/06/16/being-an-organized-executor/

Child in Office. Courtesy of Pixabay.

25. Talk to a Trust Company

If you have no reliable relatives or financially savvy friends to be the executor of your estate, consider talking to a trust company or the estate administration department of a bank. For a fee, usually based on a percentage of the value of the estate, they will carry out your final wishes as spelled out in your estate plan. They may charge a considerable sum to do this work.

Another option is to name an individual as your first choice executor, with a bank or trust company as the secondary executor, should the person you select opt out of being executor. For an ordinary individual, being an executor can be a demanding part-time job. Estate administration departments in banks and trust companies do this work all the time.

Website: http://www.investopedia.com/articles/retirement/08/trust-company.asp

Bank Building. Courtesy of Pixabay.

24. Prepare a Valid Will

A will is a legal document that a person over the age of 18 and of sound mind can create to dictate the dispersal of property and nominate a guardian for one's minor children. If you die without a will, known as intestate, each state has laws of succession that govern inheritance rights and guardianship assignments. The will names the estate executor. In most states, the document must be signed by the will's creator, with two witnesses to the signing, and be notarized.

There are online legal sites that offer free will creation forms and low-cost assistance in creating a will, but issues can be complex. Consider seeking the assistance of an estate planning attorney. Low-cost legal assistance may also be available in your town through non-profit organizations.

Website: http://estate.findlaw.com/wills/making-a-will-faqs.html

Gavel. Courtesy of Pixabay.

23. Examine Establishing a Revocable or Living Trust

Consider placing real estate properties in a revocable or living trust. Depending on the state, a revocable trust may be a good idea even if no real estate is owned. Trusts circumvent probate court involvement in property distribution, provide a quick, smooth transfer of assets to beneficiaries, and the estate's details remain private. You transfer the property's title into the trust as the grantor. It's advisable to use the services of an experienced estate planning attorney to set up a trust.

A living trust is not a substitute for a will, but it will facilitate the transfer of property. You can create a pour-over will, so that property not already deeded in the trust gets passed through the will at your death into your trust. Then those assets get distributed to the named trust beneficiaries. However, like all wills, a pour-over will must go through probate.

Website: http://www.nolo.com/legal-encyclopedia/making-living-trust-yourself-29736.html

Château de Chenonceau. Courtesy of Pixabay.

22. Review the Titling of Your Assets

Once a will and/or trust is established, keep your beneficiaries for the assets up-to-date. You may want to do this every year at tax time, when you're looking at annual statements while preparing your return. Make sure the 401k and IRA beneficiaries, annuities, insurance, investment, retirement and bank accounts go to people who are still alive and whom you still like.

Jointly held bank/investment accounts with spouses may automatically transfer to the surviving spouse, children or other named people. Some accounts, such as brokerage or retirement, are designated as Payable on Death (POD). Depending on state laws, real estate may be titled as a Transfer on Death Deed (TODD), which also avoids probate. An annual review can help you keep everything straight.

Website: http://www.abqjournal.com/743432/biz/nows-the-best-time-to-review-assets-titling.html

Office. Courtesy of Pixabay.

21. Make a Pet Trust

If you have animals that may outlive you, a pet trust ensures that they will be well cared for when you're dead or become incapacitated. You set aside money to pay for their care and name a primary, secondary and even a tertiary caregiver for your pets. Make sure these people have agreed to take your pets before naming them in your pet trust! A no-kill shelter can be one of the choices.

Collect records for your pets' vaccinations, vet visits and licensing, and keep them with the pet trust papers. And if you are already a senior citizen, avoid getting a long-lived pet, such as a parrot.

Website: http://www.aspca.org/pet-care/pet-planning/pet-trust-primer

Cat and Dog. Courtesy of Pixabay.

20. Review Royalty Income

A royalty is a payment to an owner for the use of property. This includes patents, copyrighted works, franchises or natural resources. Real estate rentals, mineral rights, oil and gas leases, and patents all generate revenue. The works of artists, authors, musicians, and other creative people may generate continuing income after the person dies.

The rock star Prince died at 57 without a will, and his estate is worth millions of dollars, thanks to both music royalties and real estate investments. Consider how royalty income will be handled after your death when making your estate plan.

Website: https://www.irs.gov/pub/irs-tege/eotopicd89.pdf

Prince. Courtesy of Pixabay.

19. Examine and Close Online Accounts

If you have online accounts that bill a credit card monthly, those charges will continue to be billed after you've kicked the bucket, until the account is cancelled. These accounts can be utilities, phone contracts, organization memberships, subscriptions, prescriptions, entertainment, travel, shopping and other services.

For the sake of your estate executor and your loved ones' sanity, examine those accounts. Close down those you don't need anymore and make a list of the ones that you keep open – and note which credit card gets billed. Keep this list with your other important papers in your Master File.

Website: https://www.everplans.com/articles/how-to-close-online-accounts-and-services-when-someone-dies

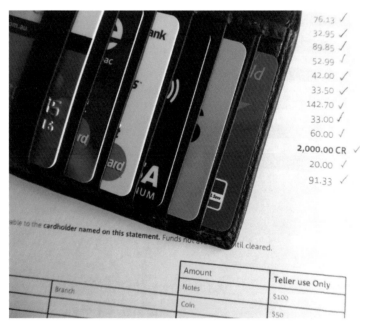

Credit Cards. Courtesy of Pixabay.

18. Identify Your Digital Executor

While you want your estate executor to be honest, organized, and financially savvy, they may not be the best person to be your digital executor. You could identify a member of the younger generation who knows his or her way around computers and the internet to handle your digital affairs. This could include shutting down social media and email accounts, retrieving online photo albums, and managing other aspects of your online life. It's helpful to pull together a listing of these accounts, user names and passwords (see Bucket List item 32).

Website: http://www.nextavenue.org/5-steps-creating-your-digital-estate-plan/

Hands on Computer Keyboard. Courtesy of Pixabay.

17. Update Your Will Periodically

Estate planning attorneys recommend revisiting your will every three to five years. As we age, relationships change, people move or die, divorce and remarriage wreak havoc on the best laid estate plans as step-children become part of the family. The most recent update of a will remains in force. However, as decades pass, you may find key people and assets in your life change. Make sure your estate plans keep pace.

Website: http://www.forbes.com/sites/lewissar-et/2013/05/22/updating-your-will-a-small-step-that-goes-a-long-way/#583a1ca8241c

Father and Child. Courtesy of Pixabay.

16. Write Your Own Obituary

One of the hardest things to do after someone dies is to write appropriate words about them for a death notice. Make it easier for everyone by writing your own obituary. You can make it funny, upbeat, inspirational or serious. To save on costs for newspaper death notices, you can keep the printed obit short and expound at length online. Many funeral homes offer online obituaries as part of their services.

Consider answering these questions: What's your exit line? For example: "(name) died, kicked the bucket, is resting with Jesus, went to the Great (Whatever) in the sky, is now playing (favorite sport) with God." What three things do you want to be remembered for? Who do you want to mention by name? Just avoid mentioning details that can be used by identity thieves with ill intent, including mother's maiden name, place of birth, date of birth and date of death.

Website: http://agoodgoodbye.com/category/notable-obituaries/

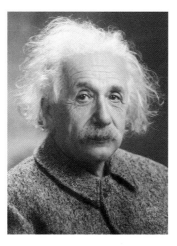

Albert Einstein. Courtesy of Pixabay.

15. Shop BEFORE You Drop

To kick the bucket on a budget, learn what you need to know before someone dies. Visit several local funeral homes to learn your disposition options and their costs. Think about it – if your car died, would you run right out and buy the first vehicle at the first dealer you visited? No, of course not. You'd do some online research, visit a few dealerships and take some test drives.

So why would you avoid doing research about funeral costs, one of the biggest expenses a family will face? It's so much easier to investigate your options while you can still laugh about death. Under duress of grief, it's no picnic, and loved ones may be tempted to overspend out of guilt and grief.

Website: https://www.consumer.ftc.gov/articles/0305-planning-your-own-funeral

Caskets. Courtesy of Gail Rubin.

14. Use Hospice Sooner, Not Later

If you or a loved one has a terminal illness, defined as a prognosis of six months or less to live, consider hospice care. It's not "giving up;" it's making the most of the patient's remaining days based on what is important to them. Many patients do so well on hospice – and palliative care for chronic conditions and long-term illness – they outlive their medical prognoses.

Too many patients endure torturous treatments that make them feel worse than the disease does, and only turn to hospice days before death. It doesn't have to be that way. Studies show hospice patients live longer and have better quality of life than those who chose to pursue aggressive medical interventions at end-of-life. Plus, hospice service costs are covered by Uncle Sam as a Medicare benefit.

Website: http://www.CaringInfo.org/ and http://www.MomentsofLife.org

Patient and Nurse. Courtesy Can Stock Photo.

13. Learn About Right to Die States

In 2014, 29-year old Brittany Maynard chose to end her battle with terminal brain cancer by swallowing life-ending medication prescribed by a doctor in the state of Oregon, where aid in dying is legal. She could not get physician assistance for a peaceful death in her home state of California.

Her death, at the time of her choosing on November 1, 2014, brought enormous attention to the topic of death with dignity, also called physician aid in dying. At the time, only Oregon, Washington, Vermont and Montana allowed doctors to legally help terminal patients achieve a gentle death. Maynard's home state of California enacted such a law that took effect in June, 2016, and many other states are considering similar legislation.

The national organizations Compassion & Choices and Death with Dignity offer information and advocacy about death with dignity and right to die laws and legislation.

Websites: https://www.compassionandchoices.org/who-we-are/ and https://www.deathwithdignity.org/about/

Dr. Jack Kevorkian, pathologist and advocate for physician aid in dying. Courtesy WikiMedia Commons.

12. Investigate Funeral Insurance Options

Average funeral costs in 2016 range from $10-20,000 – less for cremation. Many Americans don't think about saving money to pay the costs associated with their eventual demise. That is why there is insurance.

But there are so many confusing options! Funeral insurance, also known as burial insurance or final expense insurance, and those big insurance policies that cover a family's finances serve different needs. Learn your best options for your current situation by talking to an insurance agent and a funeral home's pre-need counselor.

If you already have life insurance, make sure your beneficiaries know about it. If there's no claim made when a person dies, the insurance company will not seek out the beneficiaries to distribute the money. And keep beneficiaries updated so you don't send money to an ex-spouse!

Website: http://agoodgoodbye.com/celebrant-services/funeral-insurance/

Croakem & Plantem. Courtesy of Gail Rubin.

11. Establish a Payable on Death Bank Account

Could you save $10,000 to $20,000 in the bank to cover funeral and other end-of-life costs? You can make that money easily available by setting up a Payable on Death (POD) bank account, also known as a Totten trust account. You name a beneficiary to receive these funds, and give that person the responsibility of finalizing and paying for your funeral arrangements.

You can put your funeral plans and information on file with a funeral home, without having to pre-pay. However, budget for inflation. Funeral costs went up 28% between 2004-2014, according to the National Funeral Directors Association.

Website: http://www.alllaw.com/articles/nolo/wills-trusts/using-pod-bank-account-totten-trust.html

Money. Courtesy of Pixabay.

10. Make Your Funeral Plans

Funeral planning involves many decisions that need to be made quickly. Do you want cremation or burial? What do you want done with your mortal remains? What might make a fitting tribute to your life? Do you want a religious ceremony or not? By planning ahead and outlining your ideal send-off, you can reduce stress at a time of grief, minimize family conflict, save money, and create a meaningful, memorable "good goodbye."

If you still have a plethora of objects cluttering your home, consider giving items away at your memorial service. Your loved ones bring baskets of your goods and offer them at the end, free for the taking. At the funeral of an author, her family gave away copies of her books she had in stock. Attendees get a memorial item to remember you by, and your loved ones can downsize through friends.

Website: https://www.funerals.org/frequently-asked-questions/45-four-step-funeral-planning

Memorial Marker. Courtesy of Gail Rubin.

9. Ponder Pre-Paying Funeral Expenses

If you wanted a Hollywood Viking funeral – where, assuming it could be legally done, your body is put on a boat that's set ablaze and cast out to sea – how would you ensure that happens? The best way to get the funeral you want is to pre-plan with a reputable funeral home, pre-pay the expenses, and let your loved ones know about the arrangements.

Most funeral homes will "lock-in" today's prices for the costs they control when you purchase pre-need. Make sure you buy a pre-need funeral insurance policy you own and can transfer to a different funeral home if you move. Don't write a check directly to a funeral home! It may go out of business or get bought up by another company that changes the rules after the sale. Some states use a funeral trust fund instead of pre-need insurance to protect your money.

Website: https://consumerist.com/2014/01/14/how-to-not-suck-at-pre-paying-for-your-funeral/

Viking Statue. Courtesy of Pixabay.

8. Check Cemetery Costs and Availability

Don't wait until there's a dead body in the morgue to go plot shopping! Time pressures for scheduling a funeral will make a cemetery plot search unnecessarily stressful.

Cemetery costs are in addition to funeral home fees. These include the burial plot or cremation niche, opening and closing the grave/niche, a burial vault or liner, and a memorial marker. Cemetery costs can range from a few thousand dollars to tens of thousands. Veterans and their spouses can get a free final resting place in a national cemetery.

Most cemeteries operate separately from funeral homes. Depending on your state laws, there may be more "combo" operations where you live. Unless you work with a combination funeral home and cemetery, you will interact with different people and pay different companies.

Website: http://hamilton-consulting.com/pdf/13Aug_Cemeteries_and_Mortuaries_Better_Together_or_Apart.pdf

Cemetery. Courtesy of Gail Rubin.

7. Consider Eco-Friendly Funeral Arrangements

You may think cremation is an eco-friendly disposition method. It's true you won't take up much space in a cemetery, but fire-based cremation has a sizable carbon footprint, generating an average 532 pounds of CO_2 per person (according to the Cremation Association of North America).

There's a growing interest in green burial, which focuses on placing the body in the earth as naturally as possible - using biodegradable caskets or shrouds and avoiding embalming. Jewish and Muslim burial traditions are the closest you can get to green burial in a conventional cemetery – and you don't have to be Jewish to ask for "Jewish burial treatment."

Look for more funeral homes to start offering alkaline hydrolysis, a water-based process that reduces the body to the building blocks of life at one-tenth the energy of fire-based cremation. The process also results in a greater amount of cremated remains returned to the family.

Website: http://www.agreenerfuneral.org/

Willow Casket. Courtesy of Passages International.

6. Think About Home Funerals

The Baby Boomer generation changed American culture throughout their lives, from music, to marriage, to childbirth, to aging. Now this Silver Tsunami is crashing into mortality, and many of them don't want their grandfather's funeral. Some intrepid souls are bringing funerals back into the home, where they used to be conducted before death care was entrusted to funeral directors in the 20th century.

In most states, families can do a home funeral without a professional funeral director. Family members can do the body preparations, such as washing and dressing, prior to cremation or burial. Some may help dig or fill in the grave. Family can even handle the death registration paperwork, depending on state regulations. Families who have personally taken care of their dead report feelings of healing and closure and finding deep meaning from conducting home death care and funerals.

Website: http://homefuneralalliance.org/

Still life model. Courtesy Donna Belk.

5. Get a Free Cremation

You can get a free cremation by donating your body to a local medical school. In case the school can't take the body when death occurs because there's no room at the morgue, have a Plan B in place. You can also register with an accredited national research organization, such as MedCure, the Life Legacy Foundation, or Science Care. And if anatomical donation of the body is ruled out by infectious disease, trauma, fluid retention or weight issues, have a Plan C to pay for direct cremation.

Website: http://agoodgoodbye.com/cremation/hail-and-farewell-provides-cremation-memorial-service-guidance/

Cremation Retort. Courtesy of Gail Rubin.

4. Make a Personal Contact List

When time is of the essence, can you easily assemble the names, addresses, emails and phone numbers of people who need to be contacted? Mom's dog-eared personal phone book used to hold all that information, but now cell phones, social media, tablets and computers complicate contacting the people who matter most.

Create a master contact list of information that identifies family, friends, work contacts, medical, financial and legal professionals, and other people who need to know when someone dies. Print out several copies and share with key family members.

Website: http://agoodgoodbye.com/to-die-for-shopping/the-family-plot-file-description/

Calling Contacts. Courtesy of Pixabay.

3. Write Your Famous Last Words

What would you want on your tombstone? What pithy words of wisdom would you want to share for all eternity? On my father-in-law's marker, we put these words that his father wrote to him when he graduated from junior high school. The words were written in an autograph book, framed and given a place of honor in his office: "Be good to yourself, and be good to humanity."

Me, I'm putting my public service message on my headstone: "Talking about sex won't make you pregnant, and talking about funerals won't make you dead. Start a conversation today." I hope the size restriction for the marker will still allow the entire quote to be engraved.

Website: http://www.someecards.com/news/so-that-happened/funny-gravestones-funny-epitaphs-gravestones-epitaphs/

Tombstone. Courtesy of Pixabay.

2. Talk to Your Family

Writing out your wishes is good, but talking to your family about those wishes is better. You may have indicated on your driver's license you want to be an organ donor. However, if you don't talk to your family about what you want, they can refuse to carry out your wishes if you die in a tragic automobile accident. That's why the choice is there on your license, which you should carry while you drive.

As years pass, your outlook on life and death may change. Take the opportunity to engage in casual conversations about these issues on a regular basis. It won't kill you, and your family will benefit from the conversation.

Website: http://theconversationproject.org/

Conversation. Courtesy of Pixabay.

1. Enjoy Your Life and Start Your Bucket List Today!

Without a deadline, we probably wouldn't get as much done as we do. Death teaches us to appreciate life. See the beauty in large and small ways, smell the rich aromas, savor the taste of good food, listen to nature's sounds, and touch the people you love. Go ahead and do the things you'd like to do before you die. I doubt anyone ever said on their deathbed, "I should have spent more time at the office."

Start your Kicking the Bucket List today and take action to downsize and organize. Your stuff won't do it by itself, and the people you love will thank you for removing a huge burden to carry in the midst of grief. And once you have lightened your load, you can breathe a sigh of relief, long before you breathe your last breath.

Website: http://www.lifehack.org/articles/lifestyle/25-simple-ways-enjoy-your-life.html

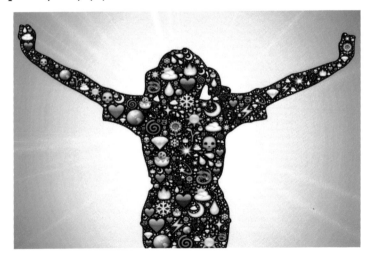

Celebrate Life! Courtesy of Pixabay.

Suggested Websites

The following organizations offer a wealth of useful information related to downsizing and organizing for end-of-life planning:

A Good Goodbye: Funeral Planning for Those Who Don't Plan to Die: www.AGoodGoodbye.com

Aging With Dignity (the Five Wishes booklet for expressing advance medical directives): www.AgingWithDignity.org

American Academy of Estate Planning Attorneys: www.AAEPA.com

American Association of Tissue Banks: www.AATB.org

Apartment Therapy (connecting people to resources to improve their homes, while reducing their reliance on stuff): www.ApartmentTherapy.com

Association for Death Education and Counseling: www.ADEC.org

Be Remembered (free site for memorialization): www.BeRemembered.com

Caring.com (senior living resources): www.Caring.com

Celebrant Foundation & Institute (Personalized life cycle celebrant training and directory): www.celebrantinstitute.org

Compassion & Choices (end-of-life education, counseling and advocacy): www.CompassionandChoices.org

The Conversation Project: www.TheConversationProject.org

Cremation Association of North America: www.CremationAssociation.org

Death Café: www.DeathCafe.com

Death With Dignity: www.DeathWithDignity.org

Donation Town (find a charity that will pick up your donations for free) www.DonationTown.org

Engage With Grace (five questions to start a conversation on advance medical directives): www.EngageWithGrace.org

Everest Funeral Planning and Concierge Service (PriceFinderSM funeral home price comparison report): www.EverestFuneral.com

Funeral Consumers Alliance (an organization dedicated to ensuring that consumers can choose a meaningful, dignified and affordable funeral): www.Funerals.org

Funeralwise.com ("Everything you need to know about funerals"): www.Funeralwise.com

Get Rid of Things: www.GetRidofThings.com

Goodwill Industries International: www.Goodwill.org

Green Burial Council (information on environmentally sustainable death care): www.GreenBurialCouncil.org

Have The Talk of a Lifetime (how to remember and honor loved ones): www.HaveTheTalkofaLifetime.org

I'm Sorry To Hear (online funeral planning tools and advice): www.ImSorryToHear.com

International Cemetery, Cremation and Funeral Association: www.ICCFA.com

In-Sight Institute (national resource for Certified Funeral Celebrants): www.InSightBooks.com

Lifehack (tips to help improve all aspects of your life): www.Lifehack.org

Life Legacy (whole body donation program): www.LifeLegacy.org

LifePosts (online commemoration of people and life milestones): www.LifePosts.com

Meaningful Funerals (why funerals and memorial services are important): www.MeaningfulFunerals.com

MedCure (whole body donation program): www.MedCure.org

National Funeral Directors Association: www.NFDA.org

National Home Funeral Alliance: www.HomeFuneralAlliance.org

National Hospice and Palliative Care Organization: www.NHPCO.org

Next Avenue (where grown-ups keep growing): www.NextAvenue.org

The Order of the Good Death (making death a part of your life): www.OrderoftheGoodDeath.com

Organized Home: www.OrganizedHome.com

Parting (online funeral home price lists): www.Parting.com

The Salvation Army: www.SalvationArmyUSA.org

Science Care (whole body donation program): www.ScienceCare.com

Selected Independent Funeral Homes: www.SelectedFuneralHomes.org

Shopping for Funeral Services, Federal Trade Commission: www.consumer.ftc.gov/articles/0070-shopping-funeral-services

Unclutterer.com (a blog about getting and staying organized): www.Unclutterer.com

U.S. Veterans Benefits: www.eBenefits.va.gov

Near Misses – An Executor's Checklist

More than 70% of adults avoid preparing for end-of-life realities. They don't have wills or trusts, advance medical directives or pre-need funeral planning in place before there's a death in the family. One way to convince people to make these arrangements is to examine the many responsibilities an estate executor has to carry out.

An executor can be a spouse, adult child, a legally-appointed friend or relative, or a trust company named by the decedent in their will or trust (*decedent* means the person who has died). The executor's job is made so much harder if information hasn't been pulled together nor decisions made in advance.

Check out this list of steps to shut down the many aspects of a life.

1. Obtain copies of death certificates.
2. Make copies of dated obituary notice and/or newspaper articles, to serve as further proof of death.
3. Meet with the decedent's attorney, as appropriate.
4. If necessary, obtain letters testamentary for executor, issued by the court that proves the authority to administer the provisions of the deceased's will.
5. Check the contents of any safe deposit boxes (requires a death certificate, executor's appointment in the will, rental agreement and photo ID).
6. Compile a list of heirs, next of kin and beneficiaries.
7. Make copies of marriage and birth certificates.
8. Review the will with the deceased's attorney to determine whether probate is needed.
9. Proceed with probate filing, if no trust was created.
10. Assemble life insurance policies.
11. Inventory tangible real estate property and locate all real estate deeds, mortgages, leases, and tax information.

12. Inventory and secure personal items such as cars, trucks, boats, recreational vehicles, mobile homes, motorcycles, furniture, fine jewelry, art and personal contents of the home(s).
13. Inventory intangible financial assets such as stocks, bonds, bank accounts, IRAs, CDs, cash, mortgages, notes, pensions, life insurance, etc.
14. File and collect insurance claims as applicable – life, medical, health, disability, travel, accident, homeowners, car and/or credit.
15. Notify those organizations providing retirement benefits, annuities and pensions.
16. Locate military records, as appropriate.
17. Locate recent income tax returns.
18. File for Social Security benefits, as appropriate.
19. File for veteran's burial and survivor benefits, as appropriate.
20. File for fraternal, union and association benefits, as appropriate.
21. File for employer benefits, as appropriate.
22. Open an estate bank account to hold money that is owed to the deceased, such as real estate rental checks and stock dividends.
23. Collect debts due the decedent.
24. Notify the Social Security Administration of the death.
25. Notify Medicare of the death.
26. Notify banks of the death and change information for any jointly held accounts.
27. Notify stockbrokers of the death and transfer ownership of jointly or solely owned stocks, bonds and mutual funds.
28. Contact credit card companies to close/cancel all individually held cards of the deceased.
29. Change all jointly held credit card accounts.
30. Examine and approve or reject claims of creditors and make payments, as appropriate.
31. Sell or transfer the title for the deceased's automobile to a beneficiary.

32. Notify creditors of the death.
33. Pass real estate and other assets owned in joint tenancy to the surviving joint tenant.
34. Transfer bank accounts and securities registered in "payable on death" form to beneficiaries.
35. Transfer funds in IRAs and retirement plans to named beneficiaries.
36. Transfer property left to the surviving spouse (in some states), or transfer assets held in trusts (such as living trusts or AB marital bypass trusts) to named beneficiaries, as appropriate.
37. Redeem/re-title government bonds, either by the beneficiary or estate administrator.
38. If the decedent had his/her own business, arrange for management of the business.
39. If the decedent was an artist, author, musician, composer, or other creative person, arrange for the continued management of royalties and ongoing sales.
40. Establish management of rental properties, both in- and out-of-state, as appropriate.
41. Terminate leases and outstanding contracts on behalf of the deceased.
42. Pay continuing expenses, such as mortgage payments, utility bills, and homeowner's insurance premiums, until a property is sold or re-titled.
43. Notify accountant or tax preparer that a final tax return will need to be prepared for the deceased.
44. Prepare and file an estate tax return for estate taxes, or any state inheritance return, if necessary.
45. Determine whether the estate qualifies for "special use valuation" under the tax laws (IRC § 2032A), deferral of estate taxes (IRC §§ 6161 or 6166), etc.
46. Pay any federal or state taxes that may be due.
47. Keep detailed records of all receipts and disbursements made on behalf of the estate, including attorneys' fees and executor's fees.

48. Keep detailed records of time spent and activities conducted on behalf of the estate during the administration of the estate.

49. When debts and taxes have been paid and all the property distributed to the beneficiaries, the estate may be formally closed by the probate court.

50. Take a deep breath and then a well-earned vacation.

When you see the many details that an executor must carry out, it becomes especially important to tackle the downsizing and organizing Bucket List items BEFORE there's a death in the family.

For a free downloadable PDF of this list, visit http://agoodgoodbye.com/kicking-the-bucket/use-this-executors-checklist-to-smooth-estate-transitions/

Yin and Yang. Courtesy of Pixabay.

Other Near Misses

Patience and Persistence: Set a goal to remove a certain amount each week, such as two boxes of material, whether it's clothes, paper, books or kitchen items.

Make Downsizing a Habit: Put discards out every week for regular trash/recycling pickup.

Do a Home Inventory with Know Your Stuff®:
www.KnowYourStuff.org

List All Your Medical and Dental Professionals Contact Information, Prescription Medications, Doses and Frequency

Boxes. Courtesy of Pixabay.

Save a Loved One's Tattoo: www.SaveMyInk.Tattoo

Dispose of Embarrassing Items Before Someone Else Discovers Them: This includes deleting old files and photos on your computer hard drives.

Make a List of People Who Owe You Money and Your Own Personal Debts

Put the Decedent's Name on the Direct Marketing Association's "Deceased Do Not Contact" List: www.IMS-DM.com/cgi/ddnc

Urn. Courtesy of Wikipedia Commons.

Let Your Executor Know Your Financial Details: If they don't know the details for the mortgage, the utility bills, the credit card companies, how can they take care of your accounts?

Keep Track of Who Gets Original Death Certificates: You can ask for the return of originals if needed.

Reduce the Hardware Collection: Recycle all those containers of old nails, screws, bolts, fasteners, washers and other hardware in the garage or basement.

Buy One, Get One Free Funeral:
www.GoodGoodbyeFoundation.org

Shopping List. Courtesy of Pixabay.

Create a Key Information Binder: Make a portable version of your Master File the family can grab and take in the event of an Emergency Room visit.

Hold a Name Your Price Yard Sale: Whatever price they say - you say OK. And if they hesitate to name a price - suggest free.

Hold a Support a Charity Yard Sale: Feature your favorite charity, say all proceeds will go towards it, and then price everything as "pay what you want."

Designate a Legacy Contact for Your Facebook Account: www.facebook.com/help/1568013990080948

Pass Goods on to Hobbyists: Model makers, ceramicists, stained glass artists, and other hobbyists, create a contact list of friends or organizations that would benefit from your collections, tools or raw materials. Note if anything is especially valuable.

Get Wood Floors Refinished: You'll have to remove everything from those rooms, including the closets. Be ruthless about reducing what goes back.

Have Your DNA Tested or Banked

Learn How Home Systems Work: Know the details of what your significant other does around the house, such as switching heating/cooling systems, doing the laundry, handling finances, maintaining a hot tub, etc.

Keep Second Choice Executors Informed: Make sure your back-up executors have copies of your estate planning documents.

Attend a Death Café: www.DeathCafe.com

Build Your Own Bucket List

1.
2.
3.
4.
5.
6.
7.
8.
9.
10.
11.
12.
13.
14.
15.
16.
17.
18.
19.
20.
21.
22.
23.
24.
25.
26.
27.
28.
29.
30.
31.
32.

33.

34.

35.

36.

37.

38.

39.

40.

41.

42.

43.

44.

45.

46.

47.

48.

49.

50.

51.

52.

53.

54.

55.

56.

57.

58.

59.

60.

61.

62.

63.

64.

65.

66.

116

67.
68.
69.
70.
71.
72.
73.
74.
75.
76.
77.
78.
79.
80.
81.
82.
83.
84.
85.
86.
87.
88.
89.
90.
91.
92.
93.
94.
95.
96.
97.
98.
99.
100.

The National Hospice and Palliative Care Organization

National Hospice and Palliative Care Organization

Hospice and palliative care offer people living with a serious, life-limiting illness expert pain and symptom management, emotional and spiritual support, and caregiver training that enables each patient and family to focus on living each day as fully as possible.

In 2015, more than 1.5 million dying Americans received care from hospice and palliative care programs across the United States. Professionals working with patients and family caregivers turn to the National Hospice and Palliative Care Organization for education, resources and information to improve the care they provide every day. NHPCO also works to help members of the public understand what high-quality care is all about and to advocate for the best care possible, especially to underserved populations including minorities, children, and our nation's veterans.

The important work being done by NHPCO ultimately means patients and families facing the journey at life's end need not do so alone. They can take that journey with a hospice team which brings comfort, compassion and hope – even in the face of death.

Learn more at www.NHPCO.org, www.CaringInfo.org and www.MomentsofLife.org.

ABOUT THE AUTHOR

Gail Rubin, CT, is a Certified Thanatologist (a death educator) who uses humor and funny films to help teach about end-of-life issues. She's known as The Doyenne of Death®. A doyenne is a woman considered senior in a group who knows a lot about a particular subject.

An award-winning speaker, she "knocked 'em dead" at TEDxABQ in 2015 (watch the video at https://youtu.be/r9qR4ZiGX2Y). She's the author of *A Good Goodbye: Funeral Planning for Those Who Don't Plan to Die* and *Hail and Farewell: Cremation Ceremonies, Templates and Tips*.

Gail is also a Certified Funeral Celebrant, a pioneer of the Death Café movement in the United States, and an informed advocate for pre-need funeral planning. She created an award-winning TV series and an internet radio program on planning for end-of-life, also called *A Good Goodbye*, and a series of radio and internet spots called *Mortality Minute*. Read more of her writing at The Family Plot Blog at AGoodGoodbye.com and in funeral trade press publications.

She's a member of the Association for Death Education and Counseling, the International Cemetery, Cremation and Funeral Association, Toastmasters International and the National Speakers Association New Mexico Chapter.

Download a free organizer/planning form and get email tips at www.AGoodGoodbye.com.

Enjoy the little things! Courtesy of Pixabay.

Praise for Kicking the Bucket List

"The connection between downsizing and death acceptance has never been more obvious. Clear your mind and conscience by sucking it up and doing the things Gail suggests."
— Caitlin Doughty, author of the *New York Times* bestseller, *Smoke Gets in Your Eyes and Other Lessons from the Crematory*.

"*Kicking the Bucket List* is a practical and fun guide that will help you get your things in order while preparing your mind and heart for the inevitable."
— Steven Waldman, founder of LifePosts.com

"This is a great, light book that helps the reader organize their life and their death. Gail has a way of making what could be a difficult task light-hearted and enjoyable! She helps the reader keep perspective and remember that the most important things in life aren't the things."
— Stephen C. Hartnett, J.D., LL.M., American Academy of Estate Planning Attorneys

"We are all moving on sooner or later -- either across town, across country or to the other side. You don't have to be terminally ill to take care of yourself, your stuff and your family affairs. Gail Rubin offers practical and not-so-widely thought-of ways of getting your "life's stuff" in order. The links to current web sites make this reference guide more expansive than the number of pages suggest."
-- Lawrence M. Mandel, Funeral Director Concierge/ Interfaith Wedding & Funeral Officiant

CPSIA information can be obtained at www.ICGtesting.com
Printed in the USA
LVIW01n0112060816
499228LV00001B/1